Table *of* Contents

Introduction

FOREWORD TO THE SECOND EDITION

Board members of nonprofit organizations operate in an increasingly complex legal environment. During the five years that have elapsed since publication of the first edition of *Legal Obligations of Nonprofit Boards*, significant federal legislation has been adopted that directly affects how board members carry out their duties. Undoubtedly the most important development was enactment of the "intermediate sanctions" provision of the Internal Revenue Code, which imposes tax penalties on individuals who derive undue personal benefits from their "insider" relationship with a Section 501(c)(3) or 501(c)(4) tax-exempt organization. However, Congress also passed the Volunteer Protection Act of 1997, through which it hoped to revitalize volunteerism by conferring legal immunity under certain circumstances on board members and others who volunteer their services to nonprofit organizations. The federal lobbying disclosure laws were revamped to require organizations that employ lobbyists (including both legislative and executive branch activities) to register and report on their lobbying activities. Amendments to the Internal Revenue Code imposed new requirements on charitable tax-exempt organizations and donors to substantiate the value of tax-deductible contributions, and increased the obligation of tax-exempt organizations to publicly disclose their federal tax returns. We have attempted in this second edition to explain the significance for board members of these, and other, legislative developments. In addition, we have added a discussion of the unrelated business income tax, which has proven to be a matter of concern to the nonprofit community, including alternatives such as forming a subsidiary corporation to carry on otherwise taxable activities.

— *Michael B. Glomb*, November 1997

*The end of law is not to abolish or to restrain,
but to preserve and enlarge freedom: for in all
the states of created beings capable of laws, where
there is no law, there is no freedom.*

— John Locke, *Second Treatise of Government*

INTRODUCTION

Nonprofit boards of directors face many challenging tasks, but ensuring the legal and ethical integrity of the organization ranks among the most critical. Ultimately, board members are responsible for protecting the organization from legal action, promoting a safe and ethical working environment, and safeguarding the organization's integrity.

With increasing scrutiny from the media and the public, board members need to be aware of the complex laws and legal principles that directly control the conduct of board members or, by regulating the activities of the organization, indirectly control the board's ability to set policy.

Most nonprofit organizations are incorporated, thus falling under the legislative and regulatory mandates for corporations. Incorporation offers added protection for individual board members. For example, an individual board member would not be liable for a corporation's debts should the nonprofit declare bankruptcy or for poor investment choices by the organization.

Nonprofit organizations usually call members of their boards *directors*. However, some nonprofits use the term *trustees*. While the term *trustee* and *director* are sometimes used interchangeably, significant differences exist in their respective legal status and obligations. For example, a true trustee is responsible for holding resources or property *in trust* for an individual or individuals and has specific, legally defined duties. This booklet does not address the obligations of trustees.

The booklet applies specifically to organizations exempt from income tax under Section 501(c) of the Internal Revenue Code. Part I of the booklet sets out established standards of conduct for board members. Part II looks at the issue of liability as it affects board members. The largest section, Part III, outlines specific requirements of corporate law, state law, and federal law affecting nonprofit organizations and, thus, nonprofit board members. Appendices include standards of conduct for nonprofit board members and tips for avoiding personal liability.

This guidebook may be used in a number of ways: as an orientation tool for new board members, as a continuing guide for experienced board members, and as a reference for executive staff. However, it is not intended to be a substitute for specific legal advice.

Part I

Principles *of* NONPROFIT CORPORATION LAW

Nonprofit board members operate within a unique legal arena. Under well-established principles of nonprofit corporation law, board members must meet certain standards of conduct in carrying out their duties to the organization. The courts usually describe these standards as the duty of care, the duty of loyalty, and the duty of obedience.

DUTY OF CARE

The duty of care describes the level of competence expected of board members. The most commonly used standard calls for board members to use the same care that "an ordinarily prudent person would exercise in a like position and under similar circumstances." Many states have statutes adopting some variation of this language explicitly for board members of nonprofit corporations. In other states, court decisions often describe a similar standard.

Board members should attend board meetings regularly, show independent judgment when voting, be informed about organizational activities, rely on trustworthy sources of information, delegate only to responsible individuals, and then follow up regularly.

Board members are not expected to make perfect judgments. They can be creative, take risks, and make mistakes without fear of being second-guessed by a court. Generally known as the *business judgment rule*, the duty of care essentially only requires board members to exercise *reasonable* care in the decision-making process.

DUTY OF LOYALTY

The duty of loyalty is a standard of faithfulness to the organization. This means that board members must give undivided allegiance to the organization when making decisions affecting the organization. In other words, board members cannot put personal interests above the interests

of the organization. Personal interests include the interests of family members as well as associated business interests.

The most common breach of this duty occurs when board members use a nonprofit organization's property for personal purposes or take personal advantage of information they obtained as board members.

Board members, their families, and their private businesses can have business dealings with the organization. However, such transactions will be subject to considerable scrutiny. Board members must fully disclose any personal interests, and the terms of any transaction must be fair. While board members generally may vote on matters in which they have personal interests, final approval should rest with a disinterested majority. State nonprofit corporation statutes frequently provide specific procedures for dealing with transactions in which board members have conflicts of interest. However, in many cases, board members should simply disclose the conflict and refrain from discussing or voting on the matter. In addition, board members should refrain from discussing confidential board business with outsiders. (See Appendix A for sample provisions for a conflict-of-interest statement.)

DUTY OF OBEDIENCE

Board members have a duty to ensure that the organization remains obedient to its central purposes. Typically, an organization's purposes are described in the articles of incorporation and other governing documents, and may be expressed in a formal mission statement adopted by the organization. Since the stated purposes may be very general, board members are usually free to exercise reasonable judgment concerning how the organization should best fulfill its mission. However, their activities must remain consistent with the central purposes of the organization since donors rely on this conceptual duty of obedience to know that their gifts will be used appropriately.

What should I do if I don't agree with a board action?

A board member who disagrees with a board action should make sure that his or her position on the matter is reflected in the board or committee minutes or other record of board actions.

Part II

Board Member
LIABILITY ISSUES

As mentioned in the introduction, one reason for incorporating a nonprofit organization is to protect individual board members and officers against personal liability for organizational obligations. Board members face two separate types of potential personal liability. The corporation and individual board members could be sued by persons who have suffered personal injury or incurred a financial loss as a result of their dealings with the organization. These are commonly referred to as *third-party actions*. In addition, a suit could be brought against board members by other board members, members of the organization, or the state attorney general seeking to hold them liable for breaches of duty to the organization (the duties of care, loyalty, and obedience). These are called *derivative actions*.

THIRD-PARTY ACTIONS

As a general rule, board members are immune from personal liability to third parties for acts of the organization. If a corporation engages in illegal or fraudulent activities, board members who directly participate in the wrongdoing may be held personally liable. Board members may also be held accountable if they failed to exercise reasonable oversight of corporate affairs that ultimately cause harm. (See Volunteer Protection Act of 1997, page 7.)

In addition, individual board members may be held liable if a nonprofit operates in a manner that demonstrates that it is not a bona fide independent organization. For example, a nonprofit organization might be determined to be acting as the alter ego or conduit for an individual or another organization. To *pierce the corporate veil* (look past the official organizational structure to the hidden operating structure), the courts will look at a number of factors: failure to maintain separate corporate records (for example, financial books and minutes of board meetings, and to observe other corporate formalities); commingling of

corporate and personal funds and assets; or use of corporate assets to support personal activities. Although piercing the corporate veil is relatively rare, in such cases, board members' failure to give proper attention to operational activities and organizational structure can have severe consequences.

Personal liability claims against board members arise frequently in the area of tort liability but are most commonly asserted in employment matters. Board members are not immune from liability if they personally participated in the wrongful conduct or failed to exercise reasonable oversight of corporate affairs that caused harm to another.

DERIVATIVE ACTIONS

Legal action may be initiated against nonprofit board members alleging that they have breached one or more of their obligations of care, loyalty, and obedience. Such actions are considered to be derived from an injury the organization itself has sustained, and hence they are called *derivative actions*.

In practice, very few parties are legally entitled to bring derivative actions, and such suits are filed infrequently. In most states, only the state attorney general, other board members, or members of the nonprofit organization may sue.

For example, board members could be sued by other members of the organization for poor investment decisions only if the investments went against good business judgment. The plaintiffs would need to show injury to the organization and prove that the board members were negligent. However, board members need to be aware that such legal actions have been successful, and courts have been known to penalize individual board members.

*C*ase Study

The board of a nonprofit children's museum decided to set up a for-profit subsidiary corporation to run a children's bookstore and use the income to help support the museum. Three board members were named as the directors of the new enterprise. Although articles of incorporation were filed with the state, nothing else was ever done to establish the store as an independent entity. All of the accounting records were kept with the museum's records. Some bookstore bills were paid by the museum. The Internal Revenue Service is now assessing back taxes and penalties against the museum, claiming that the bookstore was never a separate operation. What's more, the bookstore manager, who was fired when business slowed down, is suing the three directors who originally hired her for lost wages, claiming that they are personally liable because there never really was a separate corporation. To prevent such an outcome, the bookstore should have maintained separate bank accounts and financial records.

PRECAUTIONARY CONDUCT

Generally, as long as board members exercise ordinary diligence and care, they will not be held liable for actions or decisions that cause damage or injury, even if their decisions were the result of poor judgment. As noted previously, reasonableness is the principal test of ordinary care.

Clearly, the best way for board members to avoid personal liability is by fulfilling all of the obligations of the office — not only the general duties discussed previously, but also the specific requirements outlined in the organization's bylaws or policy statements.

Board members are not usually liable for actions taken by the board prior to their assuming office. However, they may be liable for the consequences of such actions if the actions continue during their tenure and they do not disassociate themselves from the actions. Board members should attend board and committee meetings and make their views known. They should make sure that written minutes of board and committee meetings report their dissenting vote. If board members question the propriety of corporate conduct that is not a subject of formal board action, they should make the objection known in writing.

INDEMNIFICATION AND INSURANCE

Unfortunately, even the most scrupulous conduct provides no guarantee against lawsuits. Indeed, board members are sometimes named as defendants simply to add impact to the plaintiff's case. To gain some protection against the cost of defending legal actions and the possibility of personal liability, board members may seek indemnification from their organization (where state law permits) or by assuring that the organization purchases directors' and officers' (D&O) liability insurance.

Indemnification means that the organization will pay board members' legal costs, including court judgments settlements, and attorneys' fees, for claims that result from board members' service to

*C*ase Study

Assume that the driver of a van carrying children home from a Head Start program is intoxicated and is involved in an accident causing personal injuries to some of the children. The driver and the organization, as well as the organization's board members, might all be sued. Generally, the board members as individuals would not be held liable because of the driver's negligent act. If, however, the board members had reason to know that the driver abused alcohol, or were negligent in not knowing (e.g., by failing to establish a policy requiring the program to check driving records and employment references for prospective drivers), the board members might well be found to be individually liable.

the organization. Under most state statutes, board members who have successfully defended litigation are entitled to be indemnified by the organization for the costs of defense. In many states, board members may receive payment in advance for the costs of litigation on the condition that the advance will be repaid if the suit is lost. Where indemnification is permitted by state law, the terms whereby board members can be indemnified usually are spelled out in the organization's bylaws. However, it should be noted that some state laws require that certain indemnification rights, such as the right to have expenses advanced, must expressly be provided for in the organization's bylaws in order to be effective. State indemnification statutes vary greatly, so it is important to consult with local legal counsel (who will check the relevant statute) to understand the limits of the protection provided by indemnification.

Because the organization may lack the financial resources to provide adequate indemnification or may be prevented by law from indemnifying board members under all circumstances, the organization should consider purchasing D&O insurance. D&O policies generally have two parts: reimbursement of the organization for any indemnification payments made to directors and officers, and direct payments to directors and officers when they are not reimbursed by the organization.

D&O policies often contain limitations and loopholes that can trap the unwary. It is important to check the limitations on payment per incident, per person, and in total, as well as the deductible. Policies

Can I be held liable for outstanding bills if the organization goes bankrupt?

Generally, no. Board members cannot be held personally liable for the debts of a nonprofit corporation. Although members of an unincorporated nonprofit organization and board members can be held personally liable for the organization's obligations, they are not liable for the obligations that are discharged in a bankruptcy proceeding. Note, however, that board members could be held personally liable in circumstances where the corporate veil has been pierced — that is, when a court has decided that the organization and its board members have commingled assets and activities to such an extent that it would be unfair to third parties to shield the board members from liability. In addition, some federal income tax liabilities, which under some circumstances can become the personal obligation of board members, cannot be discharged in bankruptcy.

usually provide that the insurance company must consent to a settlement, but that consent cannot unreasonably be withheld. Policies typically do not cover intentional or deliberate wrongdoing on the part of board members. In addition, it is important to check the definition of a covered loss. The cost of defense (attorneys' fees) may or may not be included within the definition of loss, and may or may not count against the total amounts payable under the policy. Plus, a policy may not protect against fines, penalties, or punitive damages.

Although board members may have concerns about the cost of D&O insurance, the alternative of self-insuring may be unrealistic, especially for members of nonprofit organizations who have extensive contact with the public and consequently face more opportunities to be sued. In light of the financial havoc that could be caused by having to defend against even one frivolous claim, D&O insurance is often worth the investment.

VOLUNTEER PROTECTION ACT OF 1997

When President Clinton signed the Volunteer Protection Act of 1997, the legal climate for volunteers in nonprofit organizations changed significantly. Designed to preempt inconsistent state laws offering varying protection to volunteers, the law grants immunity from personal liability in an effort to encourage volunteerism.

However, the new law is complex, containing numerous conditions, qualifications, and limitations. Basically, it says that volunteers would not be liable for harm if:

Should I insist on D&O insurance?

Yes. D&O insurance protects the nonprofit's assets in the event that the nonprofit is held liable for the negligent, and sometimes the intentional, acts of its board of directors and officers, and usually its employees and agents. D&O insurance may also cover board members, officers, and employees directly, or cover the organization to the extent that it indemnifies them (i.e., holds them harmless) for liability incurred as a result of their service to the nonprofit. However, a key feature of D&O insurance is that it typically covers legal expenses incurred in defending the nonprofit and the covered individuals. Without this protection, a nonprofit may not be able to afford to defend itself effectively from claims. Note that the new federal Volunteer Protection Act does not protect an organization from liability for the acts of its volunteers, nor does it protect volunteers from the costs of defending a claim. Nonprofits should be sure to review the coverage, deductibles, and other terms and conditions of D&O policies with their attorney.

- They were acting in the scope of volunteer activity.
- They were properly licensed, if necessary.
- The harm was not caused by willful or criminal misconduct, gross negligence, reckless misconduct, or a conscious, flagrant indifference to the rights or safety of the claimant.
- The harm was not caused by the volunteer operating a vehicle.

Volunteers for organizations exempt from federal income tax under Section 501(c)(3) are clearly covered by the law. Other nonprofit organizations are mentioned in the law's legislative history. It is important to note that the Act does not protect the organizations themselves, which still may be held liable for the acts of their volunteers. Moreover, while the law protects a volunteer from personal liability in situations covered by the statute, it does not protect the volunteer from being named as a defendant in a lawsuit. Ultimately, the courts will determine how the law is applied in specific circumstances. Meanwhile, board members should continue to be covered by a D&O insurance policy.

Part III

Specific
LEGAL REQUIREMENTS

A fundamental principle of corporate law holds that "management is in the board of directors," meaning that even if a nonprofit organization has paid staff, the ultimate responsibility for meeting legal requirements rests with the board. This maxim holds true for a legally incorporated nonprofit organization as well as for an unincorporated one. It is frequently cited to describe succinctly the board of directors' proper role as the ultimate policy maker for the organization.

This section outlines the major legal and regulatory requirements applicable to board members. However, because these requirements change frequently, board members are encouraged to consult with legal counsel if any questions arise.

Ordinarily, honorary, emeritus, or ex officio directors do not have a formal role in the governance of a nonprofit, and therefore are not subject to the same legal obligations and scrutiny as the other directors. Frequently, these titles are simply offered as signs of respect of special appreciation. Such directors ordinarily do not vote and are not counted in determining a quorum. However, allowing such directors to attend board meetings or otherwise to participate in the activities of the governing board may have legal consequences (e.g., the organization's attorney/client privilege). For specific advice, board members should consult an attorney.

CORPORATE LAW

A nonprofit organization's articles of incorporation and bylaws establish the legal ground rules for board members. They set the limits on what can and cannot be done by the organization and establish the rules and procedures for conducting business. For that reason, board members should be very familiar with the provisions of their organization's governing documents and be careful to act in accordance with their requirements.

These organizational documents must comply with state nonprofit corporation laws, which may dictate some of their provisions or prescribe how the corporation must handle certain matters of internal governance if the articles and bylaws are silent. Except for these state legal requirements, however, nonprofit organizations have a great deal of discretion in establishing an effective governance structure.

Board members should periodically review the organizational documents, particularly if the nonprofit grows in size or complexity or undertakes new activities. This review should determine whether the organization's governing documents continue to be appropriate or whether changes should be made. For example, starting a particularly risky activity or conducting a substantial amount of for-profit activity may call for a separate corporation as a means of insulating the existing organization from potential legal liability. (See a discussion of Subsidiary Corporations later in this section.)

A wide variety of other documents also obligate the corporation, including internal policy statements, contracts, and descriptions of the organization's activities as contained in its application for income tax exemption. Collectively, these documents establish the internal law of the organization—law as binding upon the corporation as any law passed by Congress or a state legislature.

Articles of Incorporation

The articles of incorporation, also known as the corporate charter, constitute the basic organizational document for a nonprofit corporation. The articles typically contain a statement of the organization's purposes and enumerate its legal powers and authority, including any limitations on powers. For example, in order to be recognized as tax-exempt as a charitable organization under Section 501(c)(3) of the Internal Revenue Code, the articles of incorporation must limit the organization's activities to only those permitted for a charitable organization. The charter may also contain other governance provisions, such as the method for selecting board members.

A nonprofit corporation's life begins, from a legal perspective, when the articles of incorporation are filed with the appropriate state

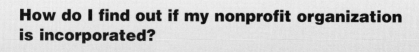

How do I find out if my nonprofit organization is incorporated?

In every state there is an agency responsible for registering and maintaining records on corporations. Usually, this agency is the Corporation Commission of the Secretary of State. Information on an corporation's status can be obtained by writing or calling the appropriate state office, which usually is listed in the telephone directory or can be obtained from directory assistance.

authority, usually the Secretary of State or the state's Corporation Commission. Once its articles are approved by the state, the corporation can only undertake activities specifically permitted by its charter. If it does anything else, it may be subject to legal challenge for exceeding its authority to act. (The technical legal term is engaging in *ultra vires* conduct.) Many state nonprofit corporation statutes, however, include broad purposes clauses that virtually eliminate the *ultra vires* problem by permitting them to engage in a wide variety of activities.

Bylaws

Bylaws are another important source of the internal law of a nonprofit organization. Because bylaws do not have to be filed with state officials, they are easier to amend and, therefore, typically provide more detailed provisions for the organization's governance.

Bylaws normally contain:

- Provisions for the selection of members and officers;

- Rules for the conduct of board meetings;

- A statement of the duties of corporate officers;

- A list of board committees and their duties; and

- A description of the board's relationship to employees and members of the organization.

Bylaws also frequently contain the organization's conflict-of-interest policy for board members and staff. (Note: *The Nonprofit Board's Guide to Bylaws*, published by the National Center for Nonprofit Boards, contains a complete discussion of common bylaw provisions. A diskette containing sample bylaws also is available.) Before changing the bylaws, board members should obtain the advice of legal counsel to be sure that proposed changes are consistent with both the articles of incorporation and state law.

Case **Study**

Nonprofit Corporation B contracted with XYZ Research, Inc., to prepare financial management software. One year later, XYZ had billed Corporation B $100,000, and Corporation B did not have a fully operational system. Corporation B sued for breach of contract and lost because the court held that XYZ had delivered a software package, which was all that the contract required. The result could have been different had the contract spelled out specific performance requirements for the system.

As an illustration, suppose that the board of directors of a nonprofit tax-exempt organization, established to act as a clearinghouse of information for parents of children with disabilities, decides to start a day care program for children with disabilities after learning that there is a need for this service. The board will first want to make sure that its articles of incorporation permit the organization to undertake this new activity, and, if not, what changes will be required. Of course, resolving any problems with the internal governance of the organization is merely the first step. As will be seen later, the board will also have to consider the income tax consequences of operating a day care center and whether that enterprise might adversely affect the organization's income tax exemption. Finally, it will have to evaluate the legal and business risks involved in providing day care to children with disabilities, examine the regulations and licensing requirements of state or local governments, and investigate the availability and cost of appropriate liability insurance.

Internal Policies and Procedures

Most nonprofit organizations, especially those with significant budgets and staff, should have written operating policies and procedures. These documents are as binding as its articles of incorporation and bylaws, and, once in place, internal policies and procedures must be honored.

These written policies could include:

- **Personnel policies**—covering employee hiring, promotion, compensation (including benefits and vacation leave), and sexual harassment and disciplinary procedures;

- **Financial management policies**—describing how organization funds are to be deposited and disbursed and identifying the person responsible for each function related to the handling of funds; and

- **Travel policies**—covering the procedures for obtaining expense reimbursement and travel authorization.

Case Study

After a year of intensive search, Nonprofit Corporation A recruited a new chief executive. At his insistence, the CEO's employment contract included six months of severance pay if his contract was terminated. A year later, the CEO left under a cloud, having overspent the budget and leaving Corporation A in financial disarray. The board refused to pay the severance, but the former CEO sued and won! The court had no choice because the contract did not contain any provision that tied the severance pay to the CEO's performance. The result would have been different had the contract provided that no severance would be paid if the CEO's contract was terminated for cause.

Having written personnel policies is a good management practice. From a legal perspective, written policies may also help a nonprofit organization defend itself against charges of discrimination, wrongful discharge, and numerous other employment-related complaints.

Courts sometimes conclude that personnel policies and other written procedures create a contract between the employee and the organization, and the organization could be held liable if the policies are not followed. The message to the board of directors is clear: Establish procedures and follow them. If a policy or procedure becomes outmoded, change the policy or procedure; do not simply ignore it.

Contracts with Third Parties

Contracts between a nonprofit organization and third parties constitute yet another body of law. An internal contract could be an employment contract with the organization's executive director or other key employees. An external contract could be with a fund-raising firm. There is virtually no limit to the number and type of contracts a nonprofit organization might have. Although board members are not usually involved in negotiating contracts, they must realize that valid contracts impose legally enforceable obligations on the organization. New board members are not free to disregard an existing contract even if the terms seem unfair or the contract appears inconsistent with the organization's mission. Their only real alternative is to attempt to renegotiate.

STATE LAW

Some state laws apply only to nonprofit organizations. Others, such as licensure and health and safety codes, apply to all corporations conducting a particular line of business, including nonprofits.

State Nonprofit Corporation Laws

Most states have statutes that govern the organization and operation of nonprofit corporations. These laws contain the minimum requirements an organization must meet to be legally incorporated as a nonprofit organization in that state, but they also affect the organization's operations long after incorporation.

For example, state nonprofit corporation laws typically require the filing of an annual report, essentially a simple form disclosing the organization's directors and officers. The consequence of not filing can be loss of corporate status with board members becoming personally liable for corporate obligations. Since some states impose sanctions on individual board members for the submission of false or inaccurate information in required reports, board members should consult with local legal counsel to ensure complete compliance.

Charitable Solicitation Statutes

State statutes regulating charitable solicitation activities are intended to prevent fund-raising fraud and abuse and to provide public information on a charity's fund-raising practices and expenses. Typically, they require a charity to register with a state agency or with the state attorney general before beginning an organized campaign to solicit contributions in that state. Sometimes, professional fund raisers retained by the organization also must register. In addition, these statutes usually require at least annual reporting on fund-raising activities, including the amounts raised and the amounts expended for fund-raising. Nonprofit organizations may be subject to fines and other penalties for violating these laws.

Other fund-raising efforts may also be subject to state law. For example, holding raffles, casino nights, or other gambling activities may require a license or permit. Similarly, selling alcoholic beverages at a fund-raising event may require a liquor license or other permit from local authorities.

State Tax Exemptions

Even if an organization is exempt from federal income taxes, it may not be exempt from paying state taxes, including income tax, corporate franchise tax, sales tax, and real estate tax. Moreover, even if a state grants an income tax exemption based on an organization's federal tax exemption, the corporation must still formally file a request for that state exemption. In some cases, state exemption requirements may be more restrictive than the federal standard.

Exemptions may be also available from other state or local taxes, such as sales tax, real estate tax, and personal property tax. Generally, a nonprofit organization must apply and qualify for these exemptions separately, and the organization must pay the tax until the exemption is approved. Board members should ensure that the organization applies for and obtains all possible tax exemptions. Otherwise, funds that could be used to carry out the organization's charitable purpose will have to be used to pay taxes.

How can we find a good nonprofit attorney?

As a general rule, "word of mouth" is a good way to find an attorney. Accordingly, asking other nonprofit organizations in your community that are involved in similar activities is an excellent way to start. Further, national associations of nonprofit organizations and national resource organizations often can provide referrals to attorneys familiar with special issues affecting nonprofits, such as tax exemption, federal grant and audit issues, antitrust law, health care law, copyright and intellectual property law. It is a good idea to talk to several attorneys or law firms to find the best "fit" for an organization's particular needs.

Licensure

States typically regulate the conduct of organizations affecting public safety or welfare by imposing licensing or accreditation standards. Common examples are health care facilities, group homes, day care centers, and educational institutions. Regulations issued by licensing and accreditation agencies can have a powerful impact on the operations of a nonprofit organization. They can prevent an organization from doing business until the organization and/or its employees meet licensing standards. Failure to apply for, secure, and renew appropriate licenses may result in monetary penalties or a complete shutdown of operations. Moreover, if a customer or client is injured and sues, the failure to have, or ensure that employees have, the necessary license can be used against the corporation in court proceedings.

Health and Safety Codes

State and local governments enact health and safety laws for the protection of patrons and employees of business establishments and other public accommodations. Nonprofit organizations are covered by these laws, and violations can result in fines or closure until the problem is corrected. Equally important, a code violation may leave the organization liable for damages to injured persons.

Charitable Immunity Statutes

Almost exclusively, state law determines the extent to which a nonprofit organization and individual board members may be held liable for damage to a third party's person or property caused by wrongful conduct. This is technically known as tort liability.

Historically, charitable organizations were not liable for such conduct under a legal principle known as charitable immunity, but that notion has diminished significantly over time. Consequently, in recent years, a number of states have enacted laws that make volunteers working with charitable organizations, including uncompensated directors, immune from tort liability.

Although these laws generally afford most volunteer board members and officers significant protection from third-party liability, the scope of protection offered varies greatly. Many laws apply only to claims involving personal injury or property damage and do not cover other potential tort claims such as libel or slander. Some provide immunity only for uninsured risks. Some do not cover board members for claims of gross negligence; illegal or criminal acts generally are not covered. Moreover, legal immunity from liability does not guarantee that board members will not be sued and incur substantial costs in defending the action. Board members should consult legal counsel to assess their potential exposure to personal liability in their state.

FEDERAL LAW

A number of federal laws affect the day-to-day operations of a nonprofit organization. Board members must be aware of the impact of these laws on the organization's activities and on their own responsibilities.

Federal Tax Law

To qualify for a federal income tax exemption under Section 501(c)(3) of the Internal Revenue Code, a nonprofit organization must be organized and operated exclusively for charitable purposes. While there is no requirement that a nonprofit organization be incorporated to qualify for exemption, the so-called *organizational test* requires that the organizational documents include provisions that limit the organization's activities to those consistent with its charitable purposes. Once approved, it is unlikely that the exemption will ever be threatened for failure to continue to meet the organizational test unless subsequent amendments to the organizing documents permit the nonprofit to undertake activities beyond the scope permitted of a tax-exempt charitable organization.

Another major consequence of an organization's tax-exempt status is that donations to charitable organizations may be deductible from an individual's federal income tax within certain limits. In addition, federal tax exemption allows a nonprofit organization to obtain grants or gifts from other charitable organizations or foundations.

A nonprofit must meet the *operational test* in order to maintain its income tax exemption. IRS regulations require the nonprofit organization to disclose any significant change in its operations that might affect its tax-exempt status. To this end, most nonprofit organizations are required to file IRS Form 990 annually. (See discussion of Form 990 under Reporting and Disclosure later in this section.)

Board members should consider the effect, if any, that operational changes might have on the organization's tax-exempt status. Whether undertaking new projects (for example, starting a profit-making venture to generate income for the nonprofit) or cutting back on existing charitable activities, the board should consult tax counsel prior to approving any substantial operational changes.

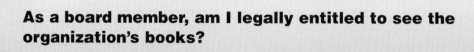

As a board member, am I legally entitled to see the organization's books?

Yes, even if the right to examine the books is not explicitly states in the organization's bylaws or other written polices. Because a board member assumes certain legal obligations for the affairs of the organization, the member has a legally implied right to the information necessary to meet those obligations. However, this right should be exercised in a reasonable manner, and at reasonable times, so as not to disrupt the organization's operations.

Private Inurement and Intermediate Sanctions

Board members should be particularly careful that their activities do not violate the private inurement doctrine. Under federal tax law, no part of the net earnings of an organization exempt under Section 501(c)(3) (charitable organizations), Section 501(c)(4) (social welfare organizations), and Section 501(c)(6) (trade and professional organizations) may inure to the benefit of any private individual or shareholder. Private inurement occurs when an organization's financial resources are transferred to an individual solely by virtue of that individual's relationship to the organization and without regard to accomplishing tax-exempt purposes. In practice, private inurement usually involves paying excessive compensation to, or engaging in unreasonable business transactions (e.g., rent, loans) with, insiders such as board members, officers, and key staff.

Prior to 1996, the only remedy available to the IRS in cases of private inurement was revocation of an organization's tax exemption. However, this was not a very satisfactory approach because those who benefited often escaped unscathed while the organization and the community benefited by the organization suffered. Accordingly, the IRS sought revocation of exemption only in the most egregious cases.

In 1996, Congress enacted legislation that allowed for a series of tax penalties, termed *intermediate sanctions*, on disqualified persons who engage in excess benefit transactions with the organization. These penalties range from a 10 percent tax on organization managers who knowingly approve the transaction to a 25 percent tax on the disqualified person, which can be increased to 200 percent of the excess benefit if it is not corrected.

Under the new law, *disqualified person* is defined as a person who benefits from a transaction and who currently is or has been in a position to exercise substantial control over the financial affairs of the organization (this can include family members of the disqualified person). The mere fact that someone holds the title of *officer* or *board member* does not of itself indicate that he or she is a disqualified person. The ability to exercise substantial influence or control is the key factor. Similarly, individuals who do not hold office in an organization can be disqualified persons if they exercise influence or control over the organization's affairs.

An *excess benefit transaction* is any transaction in which a financial benefit is provided directly or indirectly to a disqualified person if the value of the benefit conferred by the organization exceeds the value of the services or other consideration that the organization received in return for providing the benefit. Thus, board members should review compensation arrangements with key staff (i.e., those who are disqualified persons) to make sure that their compensation is reasonable. Generally speaking, compensation is reasonable if it is comparable to that paid by similar organizations for similar services to similarly qualified individuals. It is important to remember that the evaluation of reasonableness must take into account the value of all compensation received, including the value of fringe benefits and perks.

The legislative history of the intermediate sanctions legislation provides that compensation will be presumed to be reasonable if:

- The compensation arrangement was approved by the board of directors or committee of the board composed entirely of individuals unrelated to and not under the control of the individual being compensated;

How can I be sure my organization has filed the appropriate tax forms and paid all appropriate taxes?

The organization's financial managers, or its outside accounting firm, should provide a copy of Form 990 (an exempt organization's annual information return) as filed with the IRS to the board or to the board's finance and/or audit committees, if they exist. Indeed, it is good practice for the board, or the appropriate board committee, to review the Form 990 before it is filed. Similarly, copies of federal employment tax returns and Form 990 or 941 should be available and provided to the board or a board committee on request. Payment of employment taxes and the deposit of withheld employee income taxes could be reflected on the organization's financial statements, and should be reflected in the organization's general ledger and bank statements, including a record of taxes paid or funds deposited by electronic funds transfer. Failure to deposit withholding taxes for employees in a timely way can result in substantial penalties and interest assessments by the IRS, and is the most common penalty assessed against tax-exempt organizations. In some cases, directors and officers can be assessed penalties for the failure to deposit such taxes. It is desirable to have at least one outside director on the audit committee become knowledgeable of the deposit and filing requirements and monitor such activities on a monthly basis. The individual states have similar withholding and deposit requirements and can impose severe penalties as well.

- The board obtained and relied upon appropriate data in determining compensation comparability to persons in similar organizations; and

- The board adequately documented the basis for its compensation decision.

Thus, a noncash benefit — for example, a company car — would have to be treated as part of a compensation package when the board determines the reasonableness of the employee's compensation. The board cannot claim after the fact that a benefit actually was compensation if it was not treated as compensation when it was provided. In addition, an organization would need to prepare and file appropriate compensation reporting forms (W-2 or 1099). Finally, the IRS can rebut the presumption of reasonableness by providing evidence that the compensation was not reasonable. Therefore, it is extremely important that the board of directors obtain and retain adequate documentation of their compensation decisions.

Board members should review any transactions with or benefits it provides to disqualified persons, including board members. If the value of the benefits received by the disqualified person exceeds the value of what the person provided to the organization in return, a taxable excess benefit transaction may have occurred.

Unrelated Business Income

Two concerns arise when nonprofit organizations operate profit-making enterprises: unrelated business income tax (UBIT) and the potential loss of tax exemption.

Nonprofit tax-exempt organizations must pay federal income tax (at the applicable corporate tax rates) on unrelated business income. In order to be subject to UBIT, the profit-making activity must (1) be regularly carried on; (2) constitute a generally recognized trade or business; and (3) most significantly, not be an activity that is substantially related to the organization's tax-exempt purposes — that is, it must be an activity that does not contribute importantly to the organization's exempt function. For example, profits from a snack bar would be considered unrelated business income. It does not matter whether the income is used to support the organization's tax-exempt purposes.

Disputes may arise about whether a profit-making activity constitutes a bona fide trade or business and is regularly carried on. However, the main consideration in determining whether tax is due is usually whether the activity is related to the organization's tax-exempt purposes. The income tax consequences can turn on subtle distinctions. For example, the sale of art-oriented books by an art museum bookstore may be treated as being related to the museum's tax-exempt charitable purposes and, therefore, not taxable. However, the sale of toys without an art-related theme will more than likely be considered an unrelated activity and will be subject to UBIT.

Here are a few examples of common activities carried on by nonprofit organizations and an explanation of whether the IRS would consider such activities subject to UBIT.

- **Royalties** — The Internal Revenue Code specifically excludes royalties from UBIT. Although not defined in the Code, a royalty usually is considered a sum paid to a tax-exempt organization for the use of its name or other intangible asset. Thus, a nonprofit should be able to collect a fee tax-free for allowing its name to be used in connection with another business's marketing program. The tax consequences are less clear when a corporation sponsors a nonprofit organization's fundraising event or campaign. At a minimum, a corporation probably will want some recognition from the nonprofit for its financial support. If a nonprofit organization merely acknowledges such support, the IRS would likely be unconcerned. However, in the IRS's view, some forms of corporate sponsorship programs actually amount to paid advertising. In such cases, the income would be taxable. Under the Taxpayer Relief Act of 1997, *qualified sponsorship payments* are exempt from UBIT. Qualified sponsorship payments are defined as any payment made by a person engaged in a trade or business where the payor receives no substantial return benefit other than the use or acknowledgment of the payor's name or logo in connection with the nonprofit's activities. However, this safe harbor does not apply to the use of an acknowledgment of the payor's business name or logo in the nonprofit's publications or in connection with convention or trade show activities.

- **Membership List Rental/Sale** — The IRS historically has taken the position that income generated from the regular sale or rental of an exempt organization's membership list to a for-profit organization is subject to UBIT. Proceeds from the sale or exchange of mailing lists between or among charitable organizations and veterans' organizations are exempt from UBIT under the Internal Revenue Code.

What happens if I miss a board meeting?

Since board members have a legal duty to carry out their obligations responsibly, it is important that they attend board meetings regularly. Board members can be held personally liable if they are inattentive to their duties. The consequences of missing one board meeting obviously can vary according to the particular circumstances. Does the board meet monthly, quarterly, or only once or twice a year? In addition, the bylaws of some nonprofit organizations provide that a board member can be removed after missing a specified number of meetings without excuse (and sometimes even with an excuse). Board members should make sure that the minutes of meetings reflect their presence or absence, as the case may be.

- **Affinity Programs**—Similarly, the IRS frequently attempts to assess UBIT on the proceeds of an exempt organization's affinity marketing programs. In such programs, a nonprofit organization authorizes a for-profit to use its name and logo in marketing a product to the organization's members and provides access to its membership list in return for a fee. An example of an affinity program is the special Visa credit card for Smithsonian Institution members.

Taxes usually will be due if a nonprofit organization provides significant services in connection with the rental of a membership list or the promotion of an affinity marketing program. In case of a Visa card, any income generated will probably be treated as a royalty if a nonprofit organization's role is passive. However, because the legal terms of the agreement determine the tax consequences, board members should ensure a review by knowledgeable legal counsel.

A tax-exempt organization can engage in a substantial amount of unrelated business activities so long as it reports and pays the appropriate UBIT. However, if an organization fails to pay UBIT, back taxes and substantial penalties may be assessed.

Even if an organization pays the appropriate UBIT on its profit-making activities, there could still be a problem. If an organization's for-profit activities consume too much of its resources, the IRS may assert that the organization has abandoned its tax-exempt purposes for profit-making purposes and seek to revoke its exemption.

Board members, therefore, should consider the potential consequences of for-profit business activities. Again, competent legal advice is critical as the tax law regarding UBIT is relatively complex.

Subsidiary Corporations

If nonprofit organizations can generate virtually unlimited revenue from activities closely related to its tax-exempt purposes and can also engage in unrelated business activities subject to UBIT, why would a nonprofit organization need to establish a subsidiary for-profit corporation?

One reason might be that a for-profit unrelated business enterprise has grown so large that continued operation might endanger the nonprofit corporation's tax exemption. Another reason might be to protect the assets of the parent nonprofit organization. For example, many nonprofit organizations set up subsidiary corporations to handle start-up for-profit activities because of their risky nature, or to segregate particularly hazardous activities in a separate corporation.

Ownership and control of a subsidiary for-profit corporation will not endanger a parent nonprofit organization's tax exemption if the subsidiary is engaged in an independent, bona fide function and the parent is not involved in the subsidiary's day-to-day operations. If the operations overlap by sharing staff or accounting departments, for example, the IRS might determine that the subsidiary is not an independent company.

Here are some tips to prevent problems:

- Do not have all directors and officers in common. Some overlapping directors and officers are acceptable.

- Do not operate common business departments.

- Make sure that the subsidiary is adequately capitalized.

- Do not treat staff and property of the parent and the subsidiary as being interchangeable.

- Keep the daily operations of the two corporations separate.

- Maintain completely separate financial records and bank accounts.

- Make sure that the subsidiary observes basic corporate formalities, such as keeping separate records and holding shareholder and board meetings.

The role of the board member of the parent nonprofit organization is to oversee the affairs of the parent (which would include, generally, the parent's oversight of its subsidiary). The board of the parent should not be involved directly in the operations of the subsidiary or the advantages of separately incorporating the subsidiary could be lost, and the IRS (and the courts for liability purposes) could treat both corporations as though they were one. (See an earlier discussion of piercing the corporate veil in the section on third-party actions.)

Reporting and Disclosure

Obtaining an exemption from federal income tax does not exempt an organization from reporting to the IRS. With limited exceptions, such as for churches, the IRS requires a Form 990 to be filed annually. This informational return is required for organizations with annual gross receipts exceeding $25,000.

Even if an organization is not required to file Form 990, doing so

Can my personal corporation sell supplies to an organization if I serve on the board?

Generally, this is a matter covered by state law. In most states, a board member can have a personal interest in a transaction with the organization, provided that the member's interest in the transaction is disclosed to the organization, the transaction is fair to the organization, and the board member excuses himself or herself from the board's consideration of the transaction, after disclosure. Note, however, that a nonprofit organization may have established a conflict-of-interest policy that prohibits self-interest transactions entirely or that imposes substantial conditions.

will keep the organization's listing in IRS Publication 78 up to date. Publication 78, titled *Cumulative List of Organizations Described in Section 170(c) of the Internal Revenue Code*, lists organizations that are eligible to receive tax-deductible contributions, and is frequently used by potential donors.

Additional tax-related reports may be required, depending on the organization's activities. For example, an organization will have to file a Form 990-T to pay tax on any unrelated business income. (See the discussion of Unrelated Business Income earlier in this section.)

Although board members rarely are involved in preparing the tax returns (that task is typically performed by staff or an outside accounting firm), the board should at least review the returns to be sure the organization is operating in a manner consistent with its stated purposes and in accordance with the board's policies.

An exempt organization's Form 990 and application for exemption are public information. Copies of one or more of a nonprofit organization's three most recent Form 990s and its application for federal tax exemption (including supporting documents and any document issued by the IRS in response) must be made available immediately in response to an in-person request, and within 30 days of a written request. Copies must be provided without charge, except for reasonable copying and mailing costs. The IRS can assess penalties of up to $20 per day, up to $10,000, for failure to allow inspection, with substantial additional penalties for willful violations.

If I visit a member of Congress on behalf of my organization, do I have to register as a lobbyist?

No. Registration is required only for persons who are paid for their services as lobbyists, and then only if they spend more than 20 percent of their time on behalf of the organization on lobbying activities. Note that reimbursement of travel or other out-of-pocket expenses paid to a board member is not considered to be compensation for lobbying services.

Lobbying and Political Activities

As a consequence of obtaining federal income tax exemption, charitable tax-exempt organizations are limited in their ability to engage in lobbying activities, and strictly prohibited from engaging in political activities. These rules are complex, are frequently misunderstood, and have severe consequences if violated. A violation can result in loss of tax exemption and the imposition of excise tax penalties on funds improperly spent on lobbying activities.

It must be stressed that these restrictions apply to the activities of the exempt organization, not to the activities of a board member acting in his or her individual capacity. Accordingly, a board member must scrupulously distinguish between his or her personal conduct and activities on behalf of the charitable organization. For example, a board member can freely support a political candidate on his or her own time, but cannot identify the organization as supporting the candidate or use the nonprofit's telephone or stationery to solicit support for the candidate.

It is important to distinguish between *political* activities and *lobbying* activities. Political activities are defined for federal income tax purposes as intervening directly or indirectly in any political campaign on behalf of or in opposition to any candidate for public office. Nonprofit charitable organizations exempt under section 501(c)(3) of the Internal Revenue Code may not participate or intervene in any partisan political campaign activities.

Under the Internal Revenue Code, lobbying activities consist of "carrying on propaganda, or otherwise attempting, to influence legislation." In contrast to the absolute prohibition on political campaign activities, charitable organizations may engage in lobbying activities without losing tax-exempt status, provided such activities are not a *substantial part* of the organization's total activities.

The limitation on the lobbying activities of charitable organizations was added to the Internal Revenue Code in 1934. The test for what kinds of activities constitute lobbying and the amount of lobbying activities that may be conducted without endangering an organization's tax

Do I pay personal income tax on money I receive as a reimbursement of my expenses for attending board meetings?

Money received as a reimbursement for expenses is not considered to be taxable income the recipient has to account for the expenses — that is, if the board member submits a report detailing the expenses and supplying receipts, if required by the organization.

exemption have never been defined precisely, although a 1955 U.S. Circuit Court of Appeals decision suggested that legislative activities amounting to 5 percent of an organization's total activities are not substantial. The *substantial part*, therefore, remains largely subjective.

In an attempt to add some certainty to the lobbying rules, Congress in 1976 amended the Internal Revenue Code by adding Section 501(h), which permits most charitable organizations (except churches, as defined by the IRS) to elect to have their lobbying activities measured by the so-called *expenditure test*. In addition, the IRS regulations implementing Section 501(h) describe in some detail the kinds of activities that are considered to be lobbying. It must be emphasized that the Section 501(h) regulations apply only for purposes of the expenditure test. If an organization does not elect to have its lobbying activities measured by the expenditure test, the general definition of lobbying and the substantial part rule are the only guides.

Generally speaking, lobbying under the 501(h) regulations means directly communicating with a member (or his or her staff) of a local, state, or federal legislative body for the purpose of influencing the member's vote on specific legislation. Lobbying also means communicating with members of the general public in an effort to influence the vote of members of a legislative body — this is called *grassroots lobbying*.

A number of activities related to legislation are not treated as lobbying activities under the regulations. They include making available the result of nonpartisan analysis, study, or research; providing technical advice or assistance in response to a request from a governmental body; or conducting self-defense lobbying — that is, communications concerning a decision that might affect the existence of the organization, its powers and duties, its tax-exempt status, or the deductibility of contributions to the organization.

Under the expenditure test, a charitable organization may spend up to 20 percent of the first $500,000 of its exempt-purpose expenditures on lobbying activities (as defined in the regulations); up to 15 percent of the next $500,000; up to 10 percent of the next $500,000; and up to 5 percent of the exempt-purpose expenditures over $1.5 million, up to a maximum of $1 million per year in lobbying expenditures. (No more than 25 percent of total lobbying expenditures can be devoted to grassroots lobbying.)

To be certain as to which of its activities are considered lobbying and precisely what amount it can spend on lobbying without endangering its tax exemption, a nonprofit organization should consider filing with the IRS (IRS Form 5768) to elect to be covered under Section 501(h) and the related regulations.

This decision should be made only after an informed and thorough review of the benefits to be gained or lost under the election. For example, an organization that plans to engage entirely in grassroots lobbying may well be better off under the substantial part test because an electing organization is limited to spending essentially 5 percent (25 percent of 20 percent) of its exempt-purpose expenditures for grassroots lobbying, which is probably a more restrictive limitation on its lobbying program than if that same activity were measured under the substantial part test. Board members of a charitable organization engaged, or considering engaging, in legislative activities should obtain detailed information about the IRS lobbying rules, and then contact knowledgeable legal counsel for further advice relative to their specific situation.

The IRS will apply the substantial part test for any tax year for which a Section 501(h) election is not on file. An organization may revoke the election at any time (again by filing Form 5768), but the revocation must be filed before the first day of the first tax year to which it applies.

A nonprofit organization should keep detailed records of its lobbying expenditures and activities. Organizations exempt under Section 501(c)(3) must report the total expenses paid or incurred in connection with lobbying activities on Schedule A of their annual information return, IRS Form 990. While organizations that have elected the Section 501(h) expenditure test must report only the amount of their lobbying expenditures, both direct and grassroots, nonelecting charitable organizations must provide a detailed description of their lobbying activities. Apart from IRS reporting obligations, a charitable organization will need complete records in the event the IRS ever questions whether the organization has engaged in excessive lobbying activities or expenditures.

Federal tax law limits the lobbying activities only of nonprofit organizations that are Section 501(c)(3) charitable organizations. Thus, trade associations exempt under Section 501(c)(6) and Section 501(c)(4) social welfare organizations, for example, can lobby extensively without fear of losing their income tax exemption, and likewise may engage in political activity without endangering their tax exemption. Political activities may well be barred, however, under state laws or by other provisions of federal law. For example, the Federal Election Campaign Act prohibits corporations from using corporate funds to make contributions to any candidate for office in a federal election.

Note that federal grant funds may not be used either for support of political activities or for lobbying. To the extent that a nonprofit organization engages in lobbying or political activities permissible under the tax laws, it must make sure to document that these activities are not carried out with federal grant funds.

REGISTRATION DECISION TREE

QUESTION ONE*

Does your organization employ anyone who makes more than a single contact with a covered official (e.g., congressional staff member, executive branch policy maker) in a six month period?

If yes, answer question two.

QUESTION TWO

Does this person spend more than 20 percent of his or her time on lobbying activities (i.e., lobbying contacts or preparing for lobbying contacts)?

If yes, answer question three.

QUESTION THREE**

In any six-month period, do lobbying expenses for your organization exceed $20,000?

If you answered yes to *all* three questions:

ACTION NECESSARY

Register and report.

* 501(c)(3) organizations may elect to use the federal income tax law definitions of lobbying for registration and financial reporting purposes. However, reports of Houses of Congress and/or agencies contacted and issues addressed must be made by all organizations employing lobbyists.

** The lobbying threshold for organizations is indexed to the Consumer Price Index and is adjusted every four years. $20,500 is the threshold for new registrants during 1997 through 2000.

The Lobbying Disclosure Act of 1995

The Lobbying Disclosure Act of 1995 (LDA) imposed new reporting and disclosure obligations on organizations that employ a *lobbyist*. Under prior federal law, the Federal Regulation of Lobbying Act, only individual lobbyists were required to register and report their lobbying activities. Under the LDA, organizations, including nonprofits, that employ a lobbyist must register reports of their lobbying contacts and expenditures with the Clerk of the House.

Under the LDA, a *lobbyist* is anyone employed or retained for financial or other compensation who spends more than 20 percent of his or her work time for the organization on lobbying activities over a six month period. Registration and reporting are required if the organization's lobbying expenses exceed $20,000 in a six-month period. Lobbying for purposes of the LDA is defined very broadly. It includes any oral or written communication to a covered official (i.e. a member of Congress, congressional staff member, or executive branch policy maker) regarding the formulation or adoption of federal legislation; the formulation or adoption of a federal rule, regulation, or policy; the administration or execution of a federal program or policy; and the nomination or confirmation of a person subject to Senate confirmation.

Unlike the federal income tax definition of lobbying, LDA lobbying includes advocacy concerning both legislation and executive branch actions. However, the LDA applies only to federal-level lobbying; state- and local-level activities need not be reported. Similarly, as the LDA defines *lobbyist* as an individual who receives compensation, volunteer board members would not be required to register no matter how much lobbying they did on behalf of their organization.

Fund-Raising

As previously noted, state law is the primary regulatory authority of a nonprofit organization's fund-raising activities. However, the Internal Revenue Code also contains procedural and substantive provisions that affect a nonprofit's fund-raising.

Substantiating Deductible Contributions

Gifts to charitable organizations exempt under Section 501(c)(3) are tax-deductible to donors who itemize, subject to certain limitations based on their adjusted gross income. However, to be deductible, the contribution must be a true gift—the donor cannot receive anything of more than token value in return. If a donor receives something of more than token value (a so-called *quid pro quo* contribution), he or she can only deduct the difference between the contribution and the fair market value of the item or benefit received. Donors have the ultimate burden of establishing whether a contribution is deductible. However, a charitable organization that receives a *quid pro quo* contribution in excess of $75 must provide the donor with a good-faith estimate of the value of the goods or services provided in exchange for the contribution. The organization must also inform the donor in writing that the deductible amount of the contribution is limited to the amount that the donor's contribution exceeds the value of the goods or services received. The IRS may assess penalties of up to $5,000 per fund-raising event for failure to meet these disclosure requirements.

Federal tax law requires a taxpayer to substantiate deductible contributions of $250 or more. However, a charitable organization has no legal obligation to provide a donor with written substantiation if there is no *quid pro quo* contribution. (But good relations with contributors may demand otherwise!)

Employment Practices

Nonprofit organizations, perhaps to a degree greater than other private sector businesses, have a variety of work arrangements—part-time, flex-time, job-sharing, three- and four-day weeks, telecommuting, etc.—that muddy the traditional rules for determining who is an employee for employment tax purposes. Disputes related to employment issues are most likely to entangle board members in legal proceedings. While not directly responsible for supervising employees, board members can be held legally responsible if they condone illegal practices. For example, board members who knowingly allow a chief executive to discriminate on the basis of race could be sued under antidiscrimination laws.

Nonprofit organizations must obey the same employment-related laws as other for-profit organizations, including:

- The Fair Labor Standards Act;

- The Employee Retirement Income Security Act;

- Antidiscrimination laws;

- The Family and Medical Leave Act;

- Internal Revenue Code requirements for withholding employee income taxes and paying the employer's share of employment taxes; and

- Deferred compensation.

The Fair Labor Standards Act

The Fair Labor Standards Act (FLSA) is the federal wage and hour law administered by the U.S. Department of Labor. It applies to any business or organization, including nonprofit organizations, engaged in interstate commerce. The FLSA establishes the minimum wage that must be paid to certain employees and sets the rules for determining when a covered employee must be paid overtime for working more than 40 hours per week and the rate of pay. The organization's managerial and administrative personnel are exempt; clerical and other support staff are for the most part covered.

Note that covered employees *cannot* agree to waive overtime. This means that some employment practices that may be attractive to both the organization and the employee, such as compensating overtime work by allowing additional leave time instead of paying a wage premium, are not permissible. Department of Labor rules provide that the payment of a *salary* to an employee is a key element of most categories of exemptions from the FLSA. Accordingly, docking a salaried employee's pay for absences from work of less than one day is a trap for the unwary

employer. The Labor Department views docking as inconsistent with paying employees on a salaried basis, thus causing the employee to be treated as nonexempt for all purposes, including overtime pay. Employers who violate the FLSA are liable for the back wages owed, a penalty equal to 100 percent of the wages owed, interest, and attorneys' fees. Nonprofit employers should contact the local Labor Department Wage and Hour Office if there are any questions about which employees are covered or their obligations to covered employees under the act.

The Employee Retirement Income Security Act

The Employee Retirement Income Security Act (ERISA) regulates the operation of pension and health benefit plans maintained by employers for the benefit of their employees. ERISA does not require that an organization provide health or pension benefits. If an organization chooses to provide those benefits, however, ERISA is designed to ensure that pension and health benefit programs are administered fairly and that the benefits promised to employees are actually available to them when they are needed. Accordingly, ERISA requires disclosure to employees of terms of pension and health plans, provides avenues of appeal if benefits are denied, and establishes rules to ensure that highly compensated and executive employees do not get benefits out of proportion to those available to lower-paid employees.

ERISA requires a pension or health plan fiduciary to discharge his or her duties *solely in the interest* of plan beneficiaries. A *fiduciary* is defined as anyone who exercises authority or discretionary control concerning the management of the plan or the management or disposition of its assets, or has discretionary responsibility in the administration of the plan. Nonprofits typically retain outside

What should I do if I suspect a staff member is being subjected to sexual harassment?

The board member should alert the chief executive or other responsible staff person to look into the situation. The most important role that a board member can play in addressing sexual harassment, or any other employment discrimination matter, is to make sure that the nonprofit has an effective policy in place for dealing with complaints, and that the policy is followed. As board members have the ultimate responsibility for establishing policies and generally ensuring that the nonprofit complies with the law, individual members should not become personally involved in the handling of individual employee complaints.

administrators to manage their pension and health plans. However, the board of directors will be considered fiduciaries under ERISA if they retain any authority for managing the plan assets or administering benefits, rather than merely paying insurance premiums or making pension plan contributions. Because of the potential conflict of interest, board members who are also plan fiduciaries must clearly separate their role as plan fiduciaries from their roles as board members. That is, board member fiduciaries must make sure that the decisions they make as plan fiduciaries are not influenced by their position as board members of the nonprofit organization that sponsors the plan. A nonprofit board member who serves as a plan fiduciary is personally liable if he or she breaches the fiduciary duty owed to plan participants.

Antidiscrimination Laws

Nonprofit organizations are covered by federal (as well as state and local) civil rights laws prohibiting discrimination on the basis of race, sex, age, religion, nationality, and, in many cases, other protected classifications. These statutes typically prohibit the organization from discriminating in employment decisions as well as in the provision of services. Sexual harassment also is outlawed — if not in specific legislation, then by court interpretation. It is essential that board members make sure that a written sexual harassment policy exists and that it is scrupulously observed.

Under the federal Rehabilitation Act of 1973, recipients of federal grants and federal contractors may not discriminate against handicapped persons in employment opportunities or in providing program benefits or services. The Americans with Disabilities Act (ADA) enacted in 1990

How often are board members sued?

Because board members are not personally liable for the legal obligations of a nonprofit organization, they are sued relatively infrequently. One major exception, however, is in the area of employment law — e.g., employment discrimination, termination, and employee discipline matters. Employment disputes are the most frequent reasons nonprofits are sued, and board members often are named as defendants if the dispute involves a policy that was approved by the board, or should have been established but was not. Note, however, that board members can be held personally liable for their own acts such as defamatory statements, sexual harassment, or other discriminatory conduct. Moreover, while the new federal Volunteer Protection Act provides a volunteer board member with immunity from liability for conduct covered by the Act, it does not protect the board member from being sued.

extended this coverage to private employers, including nonprofits, for organizations employing 15 or more persons, and to virtually every area of public accommodation.

The Family and Medical Leave Act

The federal Family and Medical Leave Act (FMLA) establishes minimum standards for employee family and medical leave. The FMLA guarantees eligible employees, — that is, those who have been employed for at least 12 months with at least 1,250 hours of service during the preceding 12 months — up to 12 workweeks of *unpaid* leave in a 12-month period at the time of the birth or adoption of a child or at the time of a serious health condition affecting the employee or a family member. The FMLA applies to organizations that employ 50 or more persons. However, although smaller nonprofit organizations may not be covered by the FMLA, at least 30 states and the District of Columbia have family and medical leave laws with significantly lower coverage thresholds.

Employment Taxes and Withholding

Like any other corporation, a nonprofit must pay Social Security taxes under the Federal Insurance Contributions Act (FICA) and withhold income tax from employees' wages. In addition, nonprofits that are not exempt under Section 501(c)(3) of the Internal Revenue Code must pay federal unemployment insurance taxes as required by the Federal Unemployment Tax Act (FUTA). (Some 501(c)(3) organizations may be required to contribute to state unemployment insurance programs.)

The IRS can, and does, impose substantial penalties for failure to comply with employment tax obligations. Board members and administrators can be held personally liable for taxes and penalties of up to 100 percent of the taxes due. There are criminal penalties, including both fines and imprisonment, for certain willful violations. Even if your organization is in financial duress, delaying payments to the government is not a good idea.

Closely related to the obligation to collect and pay federal taxes is the matter of properly determining the organization's employment tax liability in the first place. The IRS has recently honed in on certain

Case Study

A large nonprofit organization began to have cash flow problems when contributions fell off due to a downturn in the economy. Management, with the tacit approval of the board, began to defer paying Federal Insurance Contributions Act (FICA) and stopped depositing income tax withheld from employees' wages, thinking they would make it up when contributions picked up. They never caught up, and the IRS now claims $2 million in back taxes and penalties. Some board members had their personal bank accounts attached; criminal indictments of some officers are pending.

employment practices of nonprofits. In particular, the IRS is scrutinizing the classification of workers as independent contractors, for whom employers have no tax liability, as opposed to employees, for whom employers do have a tax liability. Simply labeling a worker as a "consultant" instead of an "employee" does not dispose of the question. The IRS uses the *right-of-control test* to determine who is an employee and who is not. In simple terms, this means that if the organization has the right to control not only what the worker does but how the work is to be accomplished, the worker is an employee, not an independent contractor. Neither the job title nor the hours worked are determinative.

Deferred Compensation

Board members also should review any tax-deferred compensation for employees carefully. Virtually every 403(b) annuity plan that the IRS has audited has failed to comply in some substantial way with the tax requirements. Legislation enacted in 1996 allows Section 501(c)(3) organizations to once again maintain 401(k) plans, which had not been available to charitable organizations since 1986. While the tax law now allows additional opportunities to establish employee benefit plans, there is also an increased responsibility for the board to ensure compliance.

Antitrust Laws

Charities and other nonprofit organizations exempt under Section 501(c)(3) of the Internal Revenue Code rarely run afoul of antitrust legislation. Other nonprofit organizations, such as trade associations, have more to worry about in this arena.

Antitrust laws prevent competitors from conspiring to fix prices, drive a competitor out of business, or monopolize an industry. Because of the nature of trade associations, competitors from the same industry frequently serve on the board of directors and work together on association activities. In those cases, associations must carefully follow practices and procedures in both public and private meetings, usually determined in advance with assistance of legal counsel, to avoid violations of the antitrust laws.

Charities and other 501(c)(3) organizations usually feature diverse boards with representatives from various industries and organizations. However, it should be noted that the same antitrust provisions apply, and there is at least some potential for a violation. If, by some coincidence, board members from the same industries find themselves serving on a nonprofit board or committee together, they must refrain from any discussions or conduct that could be construed as breaking antitrust laws.

CONCLUSION

Paying proper attention to legal responsibilities is not simply a sign of good governance by board members; it constitutes the essence of the legal requirement to exercise stewardship. Like the other major responsibilities of board members, such as monitoring the organization's programs and services, fund-raising, strategic planning, risk management, and selection and performance review of the organization's chief executive officer, making sure the organization complies with corporate, state, and federal law is a critical role.

Board members can see tangible results of careful compliance. For example, the money generated through a fund-raising campaign will not be wasted on legal problems that could have been avoided, or the organization will receive an exemption from real estate taxes because board members knew that it was possible. Knowledge of their legal obligations frees board members to achieve the maximum potential from the organization's resources in pursuing its mission.

APPENDIX A

STANDARDS OF CONDUCT FOR NONPROFIT BOARD MEMBERS

A nonprofit board may wish to adopt a formal statement of conduct for members. Here are some issues that such a statement should address. Note that grants or contracts may contain conditions that require the organization to enforce certain standards of conduct in administering the grant or contract, such as antinepotism rules.

Conflicts of Interest

Statement of circumstances under which board members must disclose business and family relationships that create a potential conflict of interest; the extent to which a board member may participate in board decisions in which the member has a personal financial or other interest; and policy for retaining board members to provide services to the organization, such as accounting or legal services.

Board Member Compensation

Policy covering reimbursement of board members' direct expenses incurred participating in board activities (e.g., travel, meals) and indirect expenses (e.g., lost wages) and provisions for any direct compensation or honoraria for board members' services.

Gifts and Gratuities

Statement of policy concerning whether board members may accept gifts or gratuities from persons or organizations doing business with the nonprofit and any limitations on such policy (e.g., gifts of token value).

Political Activities

Policy statement requiring board members to disassociate the organization from any personal political activities and prohibiting using the organization's name, property, or facilities in connection with any political activity.

Hiring or Contracting with Relatives (Nepotism)

A statement of circumstances under which the organization will or will not hire persons related to board members.

Violations

A statement of consequences for violating any of the board member standards of conduct (dismissal from the board, termination of a contract, etc.) and procedures for resolving disputed cases.

APPENDIX B

TIPS FOR AVOIDING PERSONAL LIABILITY

1. Know all the provisions of your organization's articles of incorporation and bylaws relating to the organization's powers and to your authority and duties as a director.

2. Make sure that your organization complies with all federal and state laws. (Note: Violation can result in personal liability for a director.)

3. Attend board of directors' meetings regularly, including committee meetings, and keep well informed of your organization's activities.

4. Dissent on the record when you disagree with board actions, and follow up to make sure that your objection is recorded in board minutes or otherwise reflected in the organization's written records.

5. Avoid any personal or business relationships that place you in a conflict of interest with your organization or in which you have, or are perceived to have, a self-interest.

6. Make sure that the board has obtained adequate and appropriate documentation (e.g. salary comparability studies) for all employee compensation decisions.

7. Do not accept financial or other benefits from the nonprofit (or permit a family member to accept such benefits), unless the benefit is compensation for services provided, it is reasonable under the circumstances, and you did not personally participate in determining the amount of compensation.

SUGGESTED RESOURCES

Dorn, Susan E. and Zeitlin, Kim Arthur. *The Nonprofit Board's Guide to Bylaws*. Washington, DC: National Center for Nonprofit Boards, 1966, 24 pages.
   This booklet includes a checklist of bylaws contents, sample language illustrating common bylaws provisions, and a list of additional resources. Sample bylaws are also available on diskette.

Hopkins, Bruce R. *Charity, Advocacy, and the Law*. New York, NY: John Wiley & Sons, 1992, 655 pages.
   A thorough discussion of how nonprofit organizations can use charitable dollars to affect public policy lawfully. It includes chapters on federal and state regulation of lobbying and political activity and the limitations on the use of federal funds for advocacy activities.

Hopkins, Bruce R. *A Legal Guide to Starting and Managing a Nonprofit Organization*, Second Edition. New York, NY: John Wiley & Sons, 1993, 304 pages.
   A readable discussion of the basics of running a nonprofit organization, with particular emphasis on qualifying for and maintaining federal income tax exemption.

Hopkins, Bruce R. *The Legal Answer Book for Nonprofit Organizations*. New York, NY: John Wiley & Sons, 1996, 279 pages.
   Useful information for nonprofit board members presented in a question-and-answer format.

Ingram, Richard T. *Ten Basic Responsibilities of Nonprofit Boards*. Washington, DC: National Center for Nonprofit Boards, 1997, 24 pages.
   Describes the fundamental responsibilities of boards, focusing primarily on the whole board as one entity. The booklet also includes a helpful list of responsibilities for individual board members.

Kurtz, Daniel L. *Board Liability: Guide for Nonprofit Directors*. Mt. Kisco, NY: Moyer Bell Ltd., 1988, 179 pages.
   A complete discussion of board members' duties and obligations to their organizations, including an excellent explanation of board member liability insurance policies.

Oleck, Howard L. *Nonprofit Corporations, Organizations, and Associations*. Englewood Cliffs, NJ: Prentice Hall, Inc., 1980, 1221 pages.
   A complete and detailed treatment of all aspects of nonprofit association law, it nevertheless is quite readable for nonlawyers. The book contains numerous sample forms, such as sample articles of incorporation and bylaw provisions for various types of nonprofit organizations.

Sparks, John D. *Lobbying, Advocacy, and Nonprofit Boards*. Washington, DC: National Center for Nonprofit Boards, 1997, 16 pages.
   A guide to lobbying and political advocacy for board members in nonprofit organizations.

Smucker, Bob. *The Nonprofit Lobbying Guide*. San Francisco, CA: Jossey-Bass Publishers, 1991, 148 pages.
> An Independent Sector publication. The author demonstrates the many different ways nonprofits can lobby under the IRS regulations concerning lobbying by tax-exempt organizations. Specific activities that nonprofits can and cannot engage in are listed, and advice is given on applying staff and volunteer organizing skills to lobbying efforts.

Tremper, Charles. *D&O - Yes or No? Directors' and Officers' Insurance for the Volunteer Board*. Washington, DC: National Center for Community Risk Management and Insurance, 1991, 20 pages.
> This booklet examines the major issues nonprofit boards must consider when deciding whether to purchase directors' and officers' insurance. It offers explanations, recommendations, and checklists to simplify the decision-making process.

Tremper, Charles and George Babcock. *The Nonprofit Board's Role in Risk Management: More Than Buying Insurance*. Washington, DC: National Center for Nonprofit Boards, 1990, 20 pages.
> The authors demystify the fundamentals of risk management and the board's critical role in understanding and controlling the wide range of common—yet often hidden—risks that are inherent in all organizations. The booklet addresses both the need for and the shortcomings of liability insurance and other coverage in instances such as property damage, personal injury, and employee grievances.

Webster, George D. *The Law of Associations: An Operating Manual for Executives and Counsel*. New York, NY: Matthew Bender, 1990, approx. 850 pages plus appendices.
> This is a loose-leaf service updated periodically. It includes a sophisticated treatment of a wide range of issues of importance to nonprofit organizations. It is primarily a legal reference, but is of value to managers of established organizations. The volume includes a comprehensive appendix of forms.

ABOUT THE AUTHORS

Jacqueline Covey Leifer is a senior partner in the Washington, DC, law firm of Feldesman, Tucker, Leifer, Fidell & Bank. She provides counsel to nonprofit organizations on a variety of corporate issues, including development of organizing documents and personnel and financial policies; negotiation and enforcement of contracts with employees, vendors, insurers, and government agencies; corporate restructuring; capital investments; and, on behalf of organizations that receive federal grants and contracts, litigation before federal agencies and the courts. Ms. Leifer regularly teaches courses on legal responsibilities and liabilities to the boards and staff of hundreds of nonprofit organizations and state-based and national trade associations.

Michael B. Glomb is a partner in the Washington, DC, law firm of Feldesman, Tucker, Leifer, Fidell & Bank. His practice concentrates on counseling nonprofit organizations on matters affecting their tax-exempt status, internal governance, and business affairs. He has served on the board of a number of nonprofit organizations. Mr. Glomb speaks and writes frequently on legal issues of concern to nonprofit boards of directors.